KANGAROO COOKIN'

ANDREW THOMPSON is a chef of many years
experience who lives in Adelaide.

PETER WINCH is a freelance writer.

KENT McCORMACK is an artist and illustrator.

KANGAROO COOKIN'

ANDREW THOMPSON · PETER WINCH · KENT McCORMACK

Wakefield
Press

Wakefield Press
1 The Parade West
Kent Town, SA 5067
www.wakefieldpress.com.au

First published 1994
This revised edition published 2008

Designed by Dean Lahn
Printed and bound by Hyde Park Press, Adelaide

ISBN-13: 978 1 86254 326 3
ISBN-10: 1 86254 326 7

**Government
of South Australia**

Arts SA

fox creek
wines

CONTENTS

PREFACE

Kangaroo is a tasty, healthy red meat that combines well with a range of herbs, spices and vegetables. *Kangaroo Cookin'* offers 88 recipes that show how you can use roo meat both in everyday cooking and to create special meals. You'll be surprised by how kangaroo can give a 'bounce' to traditional European and Asian dishes, and how well it suits distinctly Australian fare.

The recipes create serves for four adults. They are easy to follow. Temperatures are given in degrees celsius. Most of the meals take less than an hour to prepare.

Within a month of Captain James Cook first sighting kangaroos in 1770, one was eaten by the English invaders. The Aboriginal inhabitants of Australia had been eating kangaroos for centuries, but Cook and his naturalist, Joseph Banks, thought the sight of the large macropod and the taste of its flesh worth noting.

The vegetarian roo was plentiful in all parts of the country and it became a favourite meat of early British colonists. During the 1980s kangaroo meat began to regain popularity as a free-range animal offering fat-free fillets of red meat for half the price of comparable cuts.

The Big Red, Great Western and Grey kangaroos are used for meat production. So far there is only limited organised farming of roos. They are very difficult to confine, and it is thought that the wild population is large enough to survive the controlled culling techniques. Government agencies monitor the culling of the animals and health department officials oversee the preparation of the meat for human consumption.

Only the hind quarters of the kangaroo are used. Fillets of rump, saddle (porterhouse), tenderloin and brazing or gravy steak are available. Prices for comparable cuts of beef often being three times that of roo. Specialty preparations include schnitzels, marinated kebabs and pepper steaks.

Roo has been available to butchers' shops in most Australian states for the last 20 years. The flesh is richly flavoured and dark in colour. Choosing fresh cuts is easy, as the meat tends to smell 'gamey' if it is even slightly stale.

We hope that you enjoy eating the meals we have described in *Kangaroo Cookin'* and that you have fun preparing new and unusual dishes to surprise and delight your family and friends.

SOUPS

Soups are a basic food in the cuisine of almost all nationalities. Their purpose on most menus is to stimulate the appetite, so many have a light, delicate taste and texture.

Sometimes soups are the only course in a meal. Traditional recipes from around the world create thick and chunky soups that might include noodles, vegetables and meat - a meal in a bowl!

Kangaroo is versatile enough to provide a hearty, strong meat taste for Italian minestrone style soup and can also, when cut into thin strips and treated with the right herbs and spices, offer the lightness necessary for Asian laksa. As you'll see, kangaroo even suits Moroccan soups and the soft tastes of saffron and coriander.

Most soups can be reheated, and often taste the better for it. Just make sure, if the soup contains vegetables, to boil it for at least fifteen minutes before serving again.

Make a large pot of soup on Sunday, add new ingredients as the days progress, and you'll have an easy and quick meal available all week long.

Most of our soup recipes require only an hour's cooking, and the preparation is generally straightforward.

SCOTCH BROTH

400 gms kangaroo rump or fillet, trimmed and finely diced -
2 tablespoons vegetable oil - 1 litre water - 1 large onion, diced small -
1 medium sized leek, diced small - 1 large carrot, diced small - 1/2 small
turnip, diced small - 1/2 cup fresh peas - 3 tablespoons barley -
2 tablespoons finely chopped, fresh parsley - salt and pepper to taste

METHOD

Heat oil in heavy pan, then add
the onion and roo meat. Cook
until brown, stirring frequently.
Add rest of ingredients, except
parsley and water, stir for 2
minutes.
Add water and bring to boil.
Simmer gently for about 1
hour.
Just before serving, add parsley.

SERVE

With hot buttered rolls.

MULLIGATAWNY SOUP

400 gms kangaroo rump or fillet, trimmed and finely diced - 4 tablespoons mustard seed oil (Yandilla brand is recommended) - 1 litre water - juice of 1/2 lemon - 2 garlic cloves, crushed - 1 large onion, diced small - 1 tomato, finely diced - 2 dessertspoons creamed coconut, grated - 2 dessertspoons finely chopped, fresh coriander - 1/2 teaspoon ground cardamom seed - 1/2 teaspoon ground cummin seed - 2 teaspoons curry powder - 4 curry leaves - 1 teaspoon grated, fresh ginger - 1/4 teaspoon turmeric - 1 cinnamon stick - 1/4 teaspoon ground black pepper

METHOD

Heat oil in heavy pan, then add garlic, onion, ginger, cardamom, cinnamon, pepper, cummin and turmeric. Stir and fry until onions are transparent. Add roo meat, stir, and cook for two minutes. Add curry powder and mix. Add water, lemon juice, tomato and curry leaves, bring to boil, then simmer gently for about 1 hour. Just before serving, add coconut and coriander.

SERVE

With hot chapattis.

SWEETCORN AND KANGAROO SOUP

200 gms kangaroo rump or fillet, trimmed and very finely diced -
2 tablespoons sesame oil - 1 litre water - juice of 1 / 2 lemon -
1 tablespoon light soy sauce - 1 garlic clove, crushed - 1 small onion,
diced small - small can creamed corn - 6 Vietnamese mint leaves,
finely chopped - salt to taste

METHOD

Heat oil in heavy pan, then add
garlic, onion and meat. Fry for
2 minutes while stirring.
Add corn, lemon juice, soy
sauce and water, bring to boil,
then simmer gently for 15
minutes.
Just before serving add
Vietnamese mint and salt to
taste.

SERVE

With prawn crackers.

CREAMY MUSHROOM AND KANGAROO SOUP

200 gms kangaroo rump or fillet, trimmed and finely diced -
2 tablespoons olive oil - 700 ml water - 300 ml fresh cream -
2 teaspoons butter - 1 garlic clove, crushed -
10 large mushrooms, thinly sliced - 2 teaspoons flour - 1/2 teaspoon
nutmeg, freshly grated - 2 tablespoons finely chopped, fresh parsley -
salt and pepper to taste

METHOD

Heat oil in heavy pan, then add roo meat, garlic and mushrooms, and cook for 2 minutes.
Add butter, stir, add flour and mix well. Slowly add water while stirring. Add cream and bring slowly to boil.
Simmer gently for 10 minutes.
Just before serving, season with salt and pepper, and add parsley and nutmeg.

SERVE

With crusty French bread.

Note: This soup may be blended for a smoother consistency.

KANGAROO, PUMPKIN AND GINGER SOUP

Note: For this recipe you'll need a blender.

200 gms kangaroo mince - 2 tablespoons peanut oil -
1 litre thin coconut milk - juice of 2 fresh limes - 1 clove garlic, crushed -
1/2 small butternut pumpkin, grated - 1 teaspoon grated lime peel -
2 teaspoons ground ginger - salt and pepper to taste

METHOD

Heat oil in heavy pan, then add roo meat, garlic and pumpkin. Cook for 3 minutes, stirring constantly.

Add ginger, coconut milk and lime juice, stir and bring gently to boil.

Simmer gently for 10 minutes. Blend mixture, return to pan, and gently reheat.

Just before serving, season with salt and pepper.

SERVE

Garnished with grated lime peel; pappadams are a good accompaniment.

KANGAROO SOUP WITH DUMPLINGS

200 gms kangaroo rump or fillet, finely diced - 1 tablespoon vegetable oil -
1 litre water - 1 garlic clove, crushed - 1 large onion, finely diced -
2 medium carrots, finely diced - 1 celery stalk, sliced - 1 large potato,
diced small - 50 gms self raising flour - 50 gm fresh bread crumbs -
50 gms shredded suet - 1 egg, beaten - 1 tablespoon freshly chopped thyme -
2 tablespoons finely chopped, fresh parsley - salt and pepper to taste

METHOD

Heat oil in heavy pan, then add meat, garlic, onion, carrots, celery and potato, stir and cook for 3 minutes.

Add water, stir and bring gently to boil.

Simmer gently for 20 minutes. While soup is cooking, sift flour into mixing bowl, add breadcrumbs, suet and thyme, mix them together, then add beaten egg, and stir until a dough is formed.

Roll into small balls and add to soup. Simmer for a further 10 minutes, or until dumplings are cooked.

Just before serving, season with salt and pepper and add parsley.

SERVE

With fresh, crusty bread.

BRANDIED KANGAROO AND ONION SOUP

200 gms kangaroo rump or fillet, diced finely - 2 tablespoons olive oil -
4 tablespoons brandy - 1 litre water - 2 garlic cloves, crushed - 4 large
onions, halved and sliced - 2 egg yolks, beaten until smooth and pale -
1 tablespoon freshly chopped thyme - salt and pepper to taste

METHOD

Marinade meat in brandy for at
least one hour.

Heat oil in heavy pan, then add
onions. Stir and cook on
medium heat until onions are
browned.

Add garlic, roo meat (including
marinade liquid) and thyme,
stir and cook for two minutes.

Add water, stir and bring gently
to boil.

Simmer gently for 20 minutes.

Slowly pour one ladle of liquid
from the soup into beaten
yolks, whisking until smooth.
Take soup from heat and
gradually add egg mixture,
stirring constantly.

SERVE

With hot garlic bread.

HARIRA WITH KANGAROO

*200 gms kangaroo mince - 4 tablespoons olive oil - 1 tablespoon butter -
1 litre water - 2 garlic cloves, crushed - 1 large onion, finely chopped -
1 teaspoon fresh yeast - 1/3 cup red lentils, soaked overnight and drained -
1/3 cup chick peas, soaked overnight and drained - 1/4 cup basmati rice,
soaked overnight and drained - 1 large, ripe tomato, finely chopped -
1/4 teaspoon saffron - 1/4 teaspoon ground ginger - 1/4 teaspoon
ground cinnamon - 1/2 teaspoon turmeric - 2 tablespoons finely chopped,
fresh coriander - 2 tablespoons finely chopped, fresh, flat-leaved parsley -
1 tablespoon finely chopped, fresh mint - salt and pepper to taste*

METHOD

Heat oil in heavy pan, then add
onions, roo meat, garlic,
turmeric, cinnamon, ginger and
saffron. Stir, then add lentils,
chick peas and rice. Add water,
tomato, yeast and butter. Bring
slowly to boil.
Simmer gently for 1 hour, or
until chick peas are cooked,
adding extra water if necessary.
Just before serving, add
coriander, mint and parsley.

The soup should be of a creamy
consistency.

SERVE

With fresh dates.

KANGAROO, APRICOT AND PRUNE SOUP

200 gms kangaroo mince - 2 tablespoons olive oil - 1 litre water -
1 tablespoon lemon juice - 1 clove garlic, crushed -
1 small onion, finely chopped - 1/2 cup yellow split peas - 1/2 cup dried
apricots and prunes, chopped - 1/2 teaspoon ground cummin seed -
1/4 teaspoon ground coriander - 1/2 teaspoon turmeric -
1/4 teaspoon saffron - salt and pepper to taste

METHOD

Heat oil in heavy pan, then add
onions, garlic, cummin, coriander
and turmeric. Stir and cook on low
heat until onions are transparent.
Add roo meat, saffron and yellow
split peas, stir and add water.
Gently bring to boil and simmer
for 1 hour.
Add prunes and apricots then
simmer for further 15 minutes.
Add lemon juice just before
serving.

SERVE

With warm mountain bread or
similar chunky, brown,
wholegrain loaf.

MINTED KANGAROO AND QUINCE SOUP

*200 gms kangaroo fillet or rump, finely diced - 2 tablespoons olive oil -
1 litre water - 2 tablespoons lemon juice - 1 medium onion, finely chopped -
2 garlic cloves, crushed - 1/4 cup yellow split peas, soaked overnight -
2 quinces, peeled, seeded and chopped - 1/2 teaspoon ground cinnamon -
1/4 teaspoon ground cloves - 1/2 teaspoon turmeric - 8 large, fresh mint
leaves, finely chopped - salt and pepper to taste*

METHOD

Roll diced kangaroo in chopped, fresh mint and stand for 1/2 an hour.

Heat oil in heavy pan, then add onions, garlic, cinnamon, cloves and turmeric. Stir and cook on low heat until onions are transparent.

Add meat and drained split peas, stir and add water. Gently bring to boil and simmer for 1 hour.

Saute quinces in a little oil over a low heat until cooked, add lemon juice then combine with soup. Simmer for further 1/2 an hour.

SERVE

With banana chips and spiced peanuts.

LAKSA MINT AND KANGAROO SOUP

*200 gms kangaroo rump or fillet cut in thin strips - 2 tablespoons peanut oil -
1 litre water - 2 dessertspoons light soy sauce - 1 teaspoon prawn paste -
1 small onion, finely sliced - 2 garlic cloves, crushed - 1 dessertspoon
toasted sesame seeds - 2 dessertspoons finely chopped, fresh coriander -
2 dessertspoons finely chopped, fresh, sweet basil - 3 tablespoons finely
chopped, fresh Laksa mint - 1 stalk fresh lemon grass, finely chopped -
1 teaspoon grated, fresh ginger - 1/2 teaspoon cummin seed, ground*

METHOD

Heat oil in heavy pan, then add
onions, meat, garlic, cummin,
ginger and lemon grass. Stir and
fry gently until meat is brown.
Add prawn paste, stir, and add
water and soy sauce.
Simmer gently for 1 hour.
Just before serving add coriander,
Laksa mint and sweet basil.

SERVE

Sprinkled with the sesame seeds.

HOT AND SOUR KANGAROO SOUP

300 gms kangaroo rump or fillet, trimmed and cut into thin strips -
2 tablespoons sesame oil - 2 tablespoons dark soy sauce -
2 tablespoons vinegar - 1 litre water - 1 onion, sliced fine -
2 garlic cloves, crushed - 2 teaspoons tamarind pulp -
1 carrot, sliced into thin strips - 4 tablespoons chopped spring onion -
1 small chilli, finely chopped - 4 small mushrooms, thinly sliced -
lots of fresh coriander, finely chopped - 1 teaspoon Szechwan pepper -
4 teaspoons cornflour mixed to a thin paste with cold water

METHOD

Heat oil in heavy pan, then add the onion, garlic and roo meat. Cook until brown, stirring frequently.
Add tamarind pulp, pepper, mushrooms and chilli. Stir, then add water, vinegar and soy sauce, and bring to boil.
Simmer gently for 15 minutes. Turn heat off, and thicken with cornflour mixture, stirring constantly.

Just before serving, add spring onions, coriander and carrots.

SERVE
With prawn crackers.

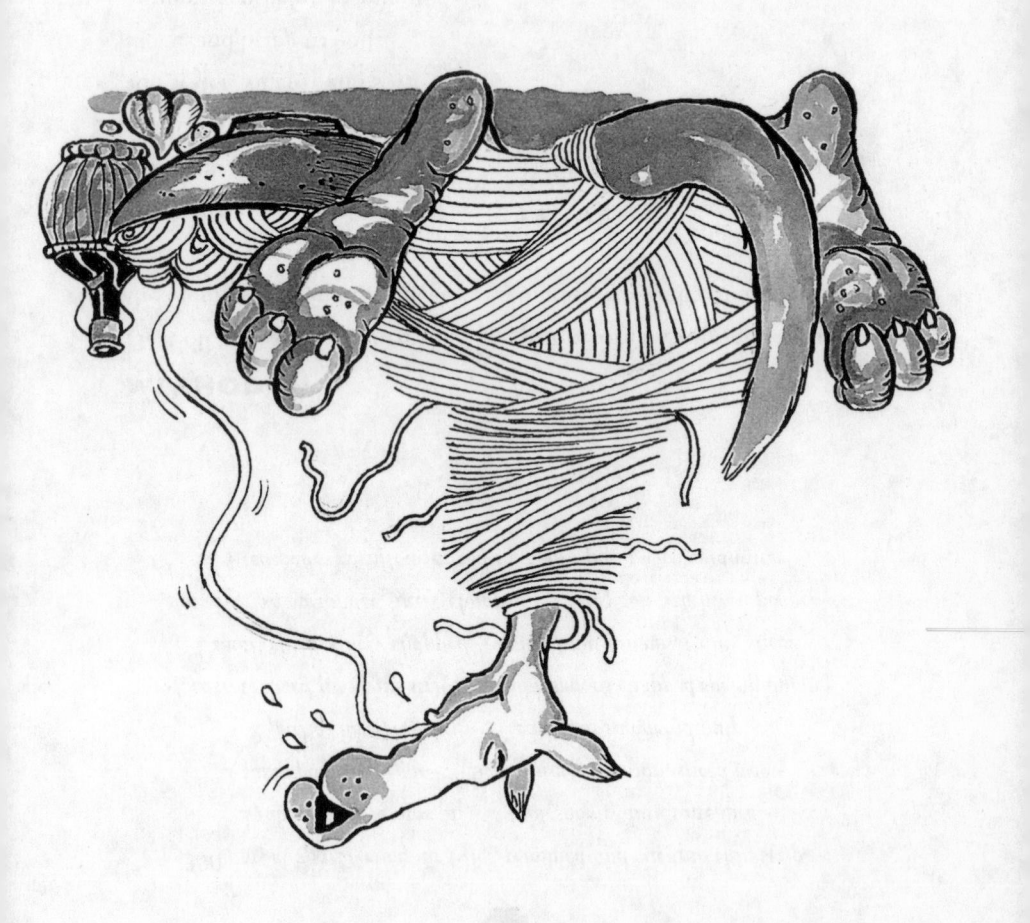

PASTA

People have cooked pasta since wheat crops were first planted. Kangaroo is a tasty, cheap and healthy ingredient in many pasta sauces.

It is simple to make your own pasta, but most people buy the ready-made product. There are a number of types on the market, all high in nutrition and low in cost, named by their ingredients and the shape of the individual noodles. There are varieties of colour and taste, made by incorporating different vegetables into the usual flour, water and egg mixture.

Dried, uncooked pasta will last in your cupboard for ages. Once-cooked pasta, smothered with your favourite sauce, can be frozen for long storage or kept overnight in a refrigerator and reheated the next day.

Cooking pasta is a simple matter of boiling it in a saucepan of water. You'll need about 2 litres of water for each 500 grams of pasta. Bring the water to the boil, then add the pasta. Stir briefly to stop the pasta from sticking, and allow to boil, usually for about 10 minutes. The best way to ensure your pasta is cooked is to begin testing individual noodles after about 8 minutes, and keep tasting until your favourite consistency is attained.

It's best to serve the noodles and their sauce immediately the pasta is cooked. Otherwise, drain the water and toss the pasta in a little butter or oil to stop it sticking together. If your pasta sticks to the saucepan while boiling, include a teaspoon of oil.

KANGAROO FLORENTINE

4 kangaroo steaks - 2 tablespoons extra virgin olive oil -
60 ml white wine - 200 ml fresh cream - 2 garlic cloves, crushed -
1/2 onion, finely chopped - 4 leaves spinach, rolled and sliced -
4 medium mushrooms, sliced - 1 teaspoon fresh oregano -
1 teaspoon finely chopped thyme - crushed black pepper to taste

METHOD

Heat oil in heavy pan, then fry steaks to desired state - rare to medium is best. Remove the meat.

Add wine and cream to pan, then add onion, garlic, herbs and pepper. Simmer to reduce liquid slightly.

Add mushrooms and spinach, then return steaks to pan and heat for 3 minutes.

SERVE

With tagliatelle and side salad.

KANGAROO SCALLOPS AND MARSALA WINE

*4 kangaroo steaks, sliced thinly - 2 tablespoons olive oil -
60 ml Marsala wine - 200 ml fresh cream - 1 garlic clove, crushed -
1/2 onion, finely chopped - 2 teaspoons fresh thyme - crushed black
pepper to taste - crushed rock salt to taste - 8 small mushrooms, whole*

METHOD

Heat oil in heavy pan, then fry
meat until browned on both sides.
Add mushrooms, onion, garlic
and fry for 1 minute.
Add wine and cream, and
simmer to reduce liquid slightly.
Add herbs, salt and pepper.

SERVE

With spinach fettucini and green
salad.

KANGAROO LASAGNE

500 gms kangaroo mince - 2 tablespoons olive oil - 60 gms butter -
200 ml water - 60 ml red wine - 250 ml fresh milk - 2 dessertspoons
tomato paste - 2 garlic cloves, crushed - 1/2 onion, finely chopped -
whole small onion - 60 gms flour - 2 eggs, hard boiled and mashed -
12 thin slices mozzarella cheese - 8 fresh basil leaves, finely chopped -
4 whole cloves - 4 teaspoons finely chopped, fresh parsley -
crushed black pepper to taste - crushed rock salt to taste

METHOD

Heat oil in heavy pan. Add chopped onions and garlic, fry until onions are transparent, then add mince. Cook for 5 minutes while stirring.

Add tomato paste and stir into meat mix.

Add red wine, water, herbs, salt and pepper, then cook on medium heat, stirring frequently, for further 5 minutes.

While mixture cools, bring milk and whole onion studded with cloves slowly to boil in a saucepan. Once boiled remove from heat. Melt butter slowly in separate pan, stir in flour to create thick paste.

Remove onion, slowly pour milk mixture into flour paste and stir vigorously to form smooth sauce. Butter casserole dish and place one layer of lasagne, precooked as per package directions, on bottom. Spoon one layer each of meat mix, white sauce, sprinkling of mashed egg and mozzarella cheese. Repeat until all ingredients used and top with cheese.

Bake in medium oven for about 30 minutes.

SERVE

With fresh garden salad.

MEATBALLS IN TOMATO AND CHILLI SAUCE

500 gms kangaroo mince - 2 tablespoons extra virgin olive oil -
2 garlic cloves, crushed - 1/2 onion, finely chopped - 1 rasher bacon,
finely diced - 2 medium cans peeled tomatoes - 1/2 cup bread crumbs -
1 egg - fresh chilli to taste - 8 fresh basil leaves, finely chopped -
2 dessertspoons finely chopped parsley - pinch of salt and pepper

METHOD

Mix meat, egg, breadcrumbs, parsley, bacon, salt and pepper, and shape into small balls.

Heat oil in heavy pan, then add onion and garlic. Fry until onion is transparent.

Add tomatoes, mashed, with juice, basil and chilli and simmer gently for approx 45 minutes.

Fry meat balls in heavy pan with a little oil.

To serve, lay meatballs on pasta and cover with sauce mix.

SERVE

With spaghetti and grated pecorino cheese.

KANGAROO ESCALOPES WITH GREEN OLIVES AND WHITE WINE SAUCE

4 thin kangaroo steaks - 2 tablespoons olive oil - 60 ml dry white wine - 200 ml water - 1 garlic clove, crushed - 8 whole green olives - 4 medium mushrooms, sliced - 2 teaspoons fresh oregano - crushed rock salt to taste - crushed black pepper to taste - 1 teaspoon cornflour mixed to a thin paste with cold water

METHOD

Heat oil in heavy pan, then fry meat until browned on both sides.
Add mushrooms, garlic and olives, and fry for 2 minutes.
Add wine and water, simmer gently for 2 minutes, then add oregano, salt and pepper.
Add cornflour mix and stir over heat until thickened.

SERVE

With vermicelli and green salad.

KANGAROO ESCALOPES WITH LEMON, ANCHOVY AND TOASTED ALMONDS

4 thin kangaroo steaks - 2 tablespoons olive oil - 60 ml dry white wine -
200 ml water - juice of half lemon - 2 garlic cloves, crushed - 1 small can
anchovies rolled with capers, drained - 2 dessertspoons toasted almonds -
8 fresh basil leaves, finely chopped - salt and pepper to taste - 1 teaspoon
cornflour mixed to a thin paste with cold water - 2 tablespoons wholemeal flower -
4 tablespoons toasted almonds

METHOD

Dust meat slices in wholemeal flour.

Heat oil in heavy pan, then fry meat until browned on both sides.

Add wine, lemon juice and water, stir, then add anchovies, garlic, basil, salt and pepper and bring slowly to boil.

Simmer gently for 2 minutes.

Add cornflour mix and stir over heat until thickened.

SERVE

With fusilli and garnish with toasted almonds.

PENNE WITH KANGAROO, PEPPERCORN, KIDNEYS AND RED WINE

*500 gms kangaroo fillet, diced - 4 lambs' kidneys, diced -
2 tablespoons olive oil - 200 ml water - 50 ml red wine - 2 dessertspoons
tomato paste - 2 garlic cloves, crushed - 1 / 2 onion, finely chopped -
2 teaspoons fresh thyme - 1 / 2 teaspoon black peppercorns, crushed -
2 dessertspoons finely chopped, parsley - salt to taste*

METHOD

Heat oil in heavy pan, then add
onion and garlic. Fry until
onion is transparent.
Add kangaroo meat and kidneys,
and cook for 5 minutes.
Add tomato paste, mix well,
then add water and wine.
Stir, add thyme and
peppercorns, then cook slowly
for about 45 minutes. More
water may be added if required.

SERVE

With penne, garnish with
chopped parsley. Side dish of
buttered green peas completes
the dish.

KANGAROO FILLET WITH SCALLOPS AND PANCETTA

4 thin kangaroo steaks - 8 fresh, whole scallops, roe on - 50 gms pancetta,
finely diced - 2 tablespoons olive oil - 60 ml dry white wine - 200 ml water -
2 dessertspoons tomato paste - juice of half lemon - 1 garlic clove, crushed -
1 small onion, finely chopped - 8 fresh basil leaves, finely chopped -
salt and pepper to taste - 2 tablespoons wholemeal flour

METHOD

Dust kangaroo slices in wholemeal flour.

Heat oil in heavy pan, add pancetta, then fry until crispy. Spoon pancetta to side of pan, then add roo meat. Cook until browned on both sides.

Add onions and garlic, then fry until onions transparent. Add wine, lemon juice and water, stir, add tomato paste and mix well.

Add basil, salt and pepper, and scallops, then simmer gently until cooked.

SERVE

With fettuccine and side salad of Cos lettuce, sweet onion rings and black olives.

SKEWERED KANGAROO FILLET
WITH PASTINI

500 gms kangaroo fillet, diced - 4 tablespoons extra virgin olive oil -
2 tablespoons balsamic vinegar - large onion, quartered and separated
into pieces - 2 large capsicums, cut into squares - 2 small zucchini cut
into thick rounds - 16 whole, small mushrooms - 4 large skewers -
8 fresh bay leaves, whole - 2 dessertspoons finely chopped, parsley

METHOD

Thread ingredients evenly onto
skewers.
Heat 1/2 of the oil in heavy
frying pan, then add filled
skewers, turning frequently to
ensure even cooking.
Lay on bed of cooked pastini,
drizzle with remaining oil and
vinegar and garnish with
chopped parsley.

SERVE

With fresh mixed salad.

KANGAROO AND AUBERGINE SPAGHETTI

500 gms kangaroo fillet, sliced thinly - 3 tablespoons olive oil -
2 garlic cloves, crushed - 1/2 onion, sliced thinly -
1 small capsicum, sliced thinly - 1 large aubergine, diced fine -
2 ripe tomatoes, finely diced - 3 teaspoons fresh oregano -
crushed black pepper to taste - 4 tablespoons grated Mozzarella cheese

METHOD

Pour oil into a heavy pan and soak aubergine pieces for 5 minutes

Heat oil and aubergines until sizzling, add onion, garlic and capsicum. Fry until onions transparent.

Add meat, and fry until browned on both sides.

Add oregano, tomatoes, salt and pepper, then simmer for 5 minutes

SERVE

With spaghetti and garnish with Mozzarella cheese.

STIR FRYING

Kangaroo is the perfect meat for stir frying. It is extremely lean, easy to slice and combines well with most herbs, spices and vegetables.

Make sure that the kangaroo fillet is cut into very thin strips and that you don't overcook the meat - the roo strips are cooked when they are browned on the outside. Use a high heat, but only for a short time, and stir ingredients vigorously so that they don't burn or char.

You don't need to use a wok to stir fry food, but it helps. The rounded base assists in the even distribution of heat and lessens the danger of overcooking. If you don't have a wok, a thick-based frying pan will do, but you may need to spend a little more time cooking. Stay close to the pan and remember: stir the food!

STIR FRY KANGAROO WITH CORIANDER AND SESAME SEED

*500 gms trimmed kangaroo fillet or rump, thinly sliced - 4 tablespoons
sesame, mustard, peanut or vegetable oil - 250 ml water - 2 tablespoons
soy sauce - 1 garlic clove, crushed - 1 small onion, thinly sliced -
hot chilli to taste - 1 small red capsicum, thinly sliced - freshly chopped
coriander to taste - 1 dessertspoon toasted sesame seeds -
1 teaspoon cornflour mixed to a thin paste with cold water*

METHOD

Poor oil into wok or heavy
frying pan.
Heat until very hot, then add
sliced kangaroo fillet.
Stir fry until 3/4 cooked - when
meat is lightly browned on
outside.
Add water and soy sauce and stir
in vigorously.
Stir in remaining ingredients.
When the mixture starts
bubbling, thicken with cornflour.

SERVE

With jasmine rice or Chinese
noodles.

STIR FRY KANGAROO WITH CANDLENUT AND ASIAN SPICES

500 gms trimmed kangaroo fillet or rump, thinly sliced - 2 tablespoons peanut oil - 250 ml thin coconut milk - 2 tablespoons light soy sauce - 8 candlenuts, halved - 1/2 teaspoon ground coriander seed - 1/2 teaspoon ground cummin seed - 1/2 teaspoon ground cardamom seed - 10 Vietnamese mint leaves, chopped - 10 sweet basil leaves, chopped - freshly chopped coriander to taste - 1 teaspoon cornflour mixed to a thin paste with cold water

METHOD

Pour oil into wok or heavy frying pan.

Heat until very hot, then add sliced kangaroo fillet.

Stir fry until 3/4 cooked - when meat is lightly browned on outside.

Add coconut milk and soy sauce and stir vigorously.

Stir in remaining ingredients.

When the mixture starts bubbling, thicken with cornflour.

SERVE

With Chinese noodles.

STIR FRY KANGAROO WITH COCONUT MILK AND FRESH GINGER

500 gms trimmed kangaroo fillet or rump, thinly sliced - 4 tablespoons
peanut oil - 250 ml thin coconut milk - 2 tablespoons light soy sauce -
1/2 onion, thinly sliced - 1/2 large red capsicum, thinly sliced -
4 snow peas, thinly sliced - 2 tablespoons fresh ginger, finely chopped -
freshly chopped coriander to taste - 1 teaspoon ground cummin seed -
1 teaspoon cornflour mixed to a thin paste with cold water

METHOD

Pour oil into wok or heavy
frying pan.
Heat until very hot, then add
sliced kangaroo fillet.
Stir fry until 3/4 cooked - when
meat is lightly browned on
outside.
Add coconut milk and soy sauce,
and stir vigorously.
Stir in remaining ingredients.
When the mixture starts
bubbling, thicken with cornflour.

SERVE

With rice or Chinese noodles.

STIR FRY KANGAROO WITH MUSHROOMS, SWEETCORN AND SNOW PEAS

500 gms trimmed kangaroo fillet or rump, thinly sliced -
4 tablespoons corn oil - 2 tablespoons light soy sauce -
4 large mushrooms, thinly sliced or diced - 1 small can of sweet corn -
12 snow peas - 2 tablespoons chopped, flat-leaved parsley -
1 teaspoon cornflour mixed to a thin paste with cold water

METHOD

Pour oil into wok or heavy frying pan.

Heat until very hot, then add sliced kangaroo fillet.

Stir fry until 3/4 cooked - when meat is lightly browned on outside.

Add mushrooms and stir for 1 minute. Drain juice from can of corn, and add juice from corn and soy sauce, stirring vigorously.

Stir in remaining ingredients, except parsley. When the mixture starts bubbling, thicken with cornflour.

Garnish with chopped parsley.

SERVE

With rice or Chinese noodles.

STIR FRY KANGAROO WITH CURRY SPICES AND YOGHURT

500 gms trimmed kangaroo fillet or rump, thinly sliced -
4 tablespoons mustard seed oil (Yandilla brand is recommended) -
4 tablespoons of yoghurt - 1 garlic clove, crushed - 1 banana, sliced -
2 teaspoons ground cummin seed - 2 teaspoons ground cardamom seed -
2 teaspoons ground coriander seed - 4 fresh curry leaves or curry powder to taste

METHOD

Pour oil into wok or heavy
frying pan.
Heat seeds and curry leaves
slowly for 1 minute, then turn
the heat up and add sliced
kangaroo fillet.
Stir fry until cooked - when
meat is brown on outside.
Spoon on top of rice, and top
with garlic and yoghurt, mixed.
Decorate with banana slices and
pappadams.

SERVE

With rice.

STIR FRY KANGAROO WITH APPLE CIDER AND SAGE

500 gms trimmed kangaroo fillet or rump, thinly sliced -
4 tablespoons vegetable oil - 250 ml apple cider - 1 garlic clove, crushed -
8 slices of fresh apple - 8 sage leaves, chopped - black pepper to taste -
1 teaspoon cornflour mixed to a thin paste with cold water

METHOD

Pour oil into wok or heavy frying pan.

Heat until very hot, then add sliced kangaroo fillet.

Stir fry until 3/4 cooked - when meat is lightly browned on outside.

Drain oil, then return to heat and stir in remaining ingredients. When the mixture starts bubbling, thicken with cornflour.

SERVE

With rice or potatoes.

STIR FRY KANGAROO WITH SESAME SEED, CELERY LEAF AND GARLIC

500 gms trimmed kangaroo fillet or rump, thinly sliced -
4 tablespoons sesame oil - 250 ml coconut milk, thin -
2 tablespoons light soy sauce - 2 large garlic cloves, crushed -
8 celery leaves, chopped - pinch of ground cummin seed -
2 tablespoons toasted sesame seeds - 1 teaspoon cornflour mixed
to a thin paste with cold water

METHOD

Pour oil into wok or heavy frying pan.
Heat until very hot, then add sliced kangaroo fillet.
Stir fry until 3/4 cooked - when meat is lightly browned on outside.
Stir in remaining ingredients.
When the mixture starts bubbling, thicken with cornflour.

SERVE

With rice and garnish with thinly sliced, long carrot strips.

STIR FRY KANGAROO WITH CORIANDER
AND SPICED PEANUTS

500 gms trimmed kangaroo fillet or rump, thinly sliced -
4 tablespoons peanut oil - 250 ml coconut milk -
2 tablespoons light soy sauce - 150 gms spiced peanuts - lots of freshly
chopped coriander and Vietnamese mint - pinch of ground cummin seeds -
1 teaspoon cornflour mixed to a thin paste with cold water

METHOD

Pour oil into wok or heavy
frying pan.
Heat until very hot, then add
sliced kangaroo fillet.
Stir fry until 3/4 cooked -
when meat is lightly browned
on outside.
Stir in remaining ingredients.
When the mixture starts
bubbling, thicken with
cornflour.

SERVE

With rice or noodles.

STIR FRY KANGAROO WITH SUN-DRIED TOMATO, BASIL AND PISTACHIO NUTS

500 gms trimmed kangaroo fillet or rump, thinly sliced -
4 tablespoons olive oil - 120 gms sun-dried tomatoes -
80 gms unsalted pistachio nuts - lots of freshly chopped basil -
1 teaspoon cornflour mixed to a thin paste with cold water

METHOD

Pour oil into wok or heavy frying pan.
Heat until very hot, then add sliced kangaroo fillet.
Stir fry until 3/4 cooked - when meat is lightly browned on outside.
Stir in remaining ingredients.
When the mixture starts bubbling, thicken with cornflour.

SERVE

With pasta or noodles.

STIR FRY KANGAROO WITH LEMON BALM AND ALMONDS

*500 gms trimmed kangaroo fillet or rump, thinly sliced -
4 tablespoons olive oil - 250 ml water - juice from 1 / 2, medium size, lemon -
2 garlic cloves, crushed - 8 leaves lemon balm, chopped - 70 gms toasted
almond flakes - black pepper to taste - 1 teaspoon cornflour mixed to a
thin paste with cold water*

METHOD

Pour oil into wok or heavy
frying pan.
Heat until very hot, then add
sliced kangaroo fillet.
Stir fry until 3/4 cooked - when
meat is lightly browned on
outside.
Drain oil, then return to heat and
add water. Stir vigorously.
Stir in remaining ingredients.
When the mixture starts bubbling,
thicken with cornflour.

SERVE

With potatoes or rice.

STIR FRY KANGAROO WITH LAMB KIDNEYS AND ONIONS

500 gms trimmed kangaroo fillet or rump, thinly sliced -
2 lambs' kidneys, finely diced or sliced - 4 tablespoons vegetable oil -
200 ml water - 4 tablespoons medium sherry - 1 garlic clove, crushed -
1 / 2 large onion, sliced - lots of chopped parsley -
pinch of black pepper, to taste - 1 teaspoon cornflour mixed to a thin
paste with cold water

METHOD

Pour oil into wok or heavy frying pan.

Heat until very hot, then add kidneys and sliced kangaroo fillet. Stir fry until 3/4 cooked - when meat is lightly browned on outside.

Drain oil, then return to heat and add water, sherry, pepper, garlic, onion and 1/2 of the chopped parsley, stirring vigorously.

When bubbling, thicken with cornflour.

SERVE

With mashed potatoes and garnish with remaining parsley.

STIR FRY KANGAROO IN OYSTER AND STOUT SAUCE

500 gms trimmed kangaroo fillet or rump, thinly sliced - 8 fresh oysters - 4 tablespoons vegetable oil - 250 ml stout - 1 teaspoon Worcestershire sauce - 2 garlic cloves, crushed - 1 small onion, thinly sliced - 2 tablespoons parsley, finely chopped - black pepper to taste - 1 teaspoon cornflour mixed to a thin paste with cold water

METHOD

Pour oil into wok or heavy frying pan.

Heat until very hot, then add sliced kangaroo fillet.

Stir fry until 3/4 cooked - when meat is lightly browned on outside.

Drain oil, then return to heat, add stout and remaining ingredients, and stir vigorously. When bubbling, thicken with cornflour.

SERVE

With mashed potatoes or rice.

MOROCCAN STIR FRY KANGAROO

500 gms trimmed kangaroo fillet or rump, thinly sliced -
4 tablespoons olive oil - juice of 1 lemon - 8 dessertspoons yoghurt -
2 cloves garlic, crushed - 1 large zucchini, sliced, not too thin -
1 large, red capsicum, cut into small squares - 1 small onion, quartered -
8 leaves fresh basil, finely chopped - 1 / 2 teaspoon saffron -
1 teaspoon ground cummin seed - 1 / 2 teaspoon ground ginger -
8 leaves fresh mint, finely chopped - 1 teaspoon cornflour mixed to a thin
paste with cold water

METHOD

Pour oil into wok or heavy
frying pan.
Heat until very hot, then add
sliced kangaroo fillet and saffron.
Stir fry until 3/4 cooked -
when meat is lightly browned
on outside.
Stir in remaining ingredients,
except yoghurt and mint. When
the mixture starts bubbling,
thicken with cornflour.
Mix yoghurt and mint together.

SERVE

With rice or couscous topped
with yoghurt and mint mix.

STIR FRY KANGAROO WITH CORIANDER AND CHILLI

500 gms trimmed kangaroo fillet or rump, thinly sliced -
4 tablespoons peanut or sesame oil - 250 ml coconut milk, thin -
2 tablespoons light soy sauce - 2 garlic cloves, crushed - small tin bamboo
shoots, drained - 4 small, fresh red chillies, finely chopped -
lots of fresh coriander, chopped - 1 stalk fresh lemon grass, finely sliced -
1 teaspoon cornflour mixed to a thin paste with cold water

METHOD

Note: this dish is very hot.

Pour oil into wok or heavy
frying pan.
Heat until very hot, then add
sliced kangaroo fillet.
Stir fry until 3/4 cooked - when
meat is lightly browned on
outside.
Stir in remaining ingredients.
When the mixture starts
bubbling, thicken with cornflour.

SERVE

With Chinese noodles.

STIR FRY KANGAROO WITH PRAWN AND WATER CHESTNUTS

500 gms trimmed kangaroo fillet or rump, thinly sliced -
4 tablespoons peanut or sesame oil - 250 ml thin coconut milk -
2 tablespoons light soy sauce - 2 cloves garlic, crushed - 8 large, green
prawns, halved lengthways - 1 large handful fresh bean sprouts -
1 small can water chestnuts, drained and halved - 12 leaves fresh, sweet
basil, finely chopped - 1 teaspoon cornflour mixed to a thin paste with
cold water

METHOD

Pour oil into wok or heavy
frying pan.
Heat until very hot, then add
sliced kangaroo fillet.
Stir fry until 3/4 cooked -
when meat is lightly browned
on outside.
Stir in remaining ingredients.
When the mixture starts
bubbling, thicken with
cornflour.

SERVE

With Chinese noodles or rice.

MILD SPICED KANGAROO WITH BANANA AND COCONUT MILK

800 gms trimmed kangaroo fillet or rump, thinly sliced -
4 tablespoons peanut oil - 250 ml coconut milk - 1 garlic clove, crushed -
1 small onion, thinly sliced - 1 ripe tomato, diced -
4 slices of banana per person - 6 curry leaves -
1 teaspoon ground cardamom - 1 teaspoon ground cummin seed -
1 teaspoon ground coriander seed - 2 dessertspoons fresh chopped coriander -
4 dessertspoons of yoghurt

METHOD

Pour oil into wok or heavy frying pan. Heat until very hot, then add sliced kangaroo fillet and curry leaves. Stir fry until 3/4 cooked - when meat is lightly browned on outside. Add onion, garlic and cardamom, cummin and coriander seeds. Stir in tomatoes, coconut milk and banana. Simmer for 2 minutes, stirring all the time.

SERVE

With jasmine rice, garnished with fresh coriander and yoghurt.

CHAR GRILLING

Cooks knew from ancient times that food tasted better if it was suspended close to the hot coals of a fire. These days, the humble griller on your stove serves as a good substitute.

In Australia, kangaroo fillets are the most economical form of tender, fat-free meat for grilling, and the flesh has the perfect texture to absorb tastes from dry and wet seasoning. You can produce any number of tastes by char grilling roo that has been marinated in herbs, oils and spices: the perfect meal to impress dinner guests and maintain variety for your family and friends.

First sear the fillets on both sides at a high temperature to seal the flesh and contain the flavoursome juices. Lower the heat and turn the fillets frequently to ensure the meat is cooked to a consistent texture.

The easiest way to check when the roo is rare, medium or well-done is by the softness of the fillet: rare meat is very soft and springy to the touch, while well-done meat is quite hard and stiff.

Our recipes can also be used for barbequed or pan-fried meals.

CHAR GRILLED KANGAROO FILLET WITH LEMON AND BLACK PEPPER SAUCE

4 fillets of kangaroo, about 200 gms each - 250 ml water -
juice of 1 lemon - 1 garlic clove, crushed - 1 tablespoon chopped parsley -
crushed black peppercorns to taste - 1 teaspoon cornflour mixed to a thin
paste with cold water

METHOD

Char grill fillets to desired state.
While fillets are cooking, bring
water to boil, then add
peppercorns, lemon juice and
garlic. Turn down to simmer.
When fillets are cooked, add to
the simmering sauce. Leave for a
minute or two to allow some
juices to flavour the sauce, then
thicken sauce with cornflour.
Just before serving, season with
salt (if desired) and add parsley.

SERVE

With rice or potatoes.

CHAR GRILLED KANGAROO FILLET WITH WILD ROSELLA FLOWER AND NATIVE PEPPER LEAF

4 fillets of kangaroo, about 200 gms each - 250 ml water -
8 rosella flowers - 4 native pepper leaves -
1 teaspoon cornflour mixed to a thin paste with cold water

METHOD

Make a small pocket in centre of each fillet and insert 1 rosella flower.

Char grill fillets to desired state. While fillets are cooking, heat stock, add remaining rosella flowers and pepper leaves.

When fillets are cooked, add to the stock. Leave for a minute or two to allow some juices to flavour the sauce, then thicken sauce with cornflour.

SERVE

With brown rice or potatoes.

CHAR GRILLED KANGAROO FILLET WITH A LIGHT MUSTARD AND PEAR SAUCE

4 fillets of kangaroo, about 200 gms each - 250 ml cream - 50 ml pear or apple juice - 2 dessertspoons Australian mustard - 8 thin slices fresh pear - 1 dessertspoon chopped chives or spring onions

METHOD

Char grill fillets to desired state. While fillets are cooking, pour cream, pear or apple juice and mustard into a heavy pan, then mix. Bring to the boil and turn down to simmer until sauce thickens.

When fillets are cooked, add to sauce, leave for a minute or two to allow some juices to flavour the sauce, then add pear slices. Garnish with chives or spring onions

SERVE

With rice or potatoes.

CHAR GRILLED KANGAROO FILLET WITH CREAMY MUSHROOM AND GREEN PEPPERCORN SAUCE

4 fillets of kangaroo, about 200 gms each - 250 ml cream -
50 ml brandy - 1 garlic clove, crushed - 2 dessertspoons green peppercorns -
1 dessertspoon chopped chives or spring onions

METHOD

Char grill fillets to desired state. While fillets are cooking, pour cream, brandy, peppercorns and garlic into a heavy pan, then mix. Bring to the boil and turn down to simmer until sauce thickens.

When fillets are cooked, add to sauce, leave for a minute or two to allow some juices to flavour the sauce.

Garnish with chives or spring onions.

SERVE

With rice or potatoes.

CHAR GRILLED KANGAROO FILLET WITH DRAMBUIE, LEEK AND OATMEAL SAUCE

4 fillets of kangaroo, about 200 gms each - 30 ml Drambuie -
250 ml fresh cream - 1/2 small leek, sliced -
1 tablespoon toasted oatmeal - 1 tablespoon finely chopped, fresh parsley -
black pepper to taste

METHOD

Char grill fillets to desired state.
While fillets are cooking, pour
cream into a heavy pan, add
leek, oatmeal and Drambuie,
then heat to reduce slightly.
When fillets are cooked, add to
mixture, leave for a minute or
two to allow some juices to
flavour the sauce, then add
pepper.
Garnish with fresh parsley.

SERVE

With mashed potatoes.

CHAR GRILLED KANGAROO FILLET WITH
GARLIC AND WHITE WINE SAUCE

4 fillets of kangaroo, about 200 gms each -
2 tablespoons extra virgin olive oil - 250 ml fresh cream -
50 ml dry white wine - 4 garlic cloves, crushed -
6 fresh basil leaves, chopped - black pepper to taste

METHOD

Char grill fillets to desired state.
While fillets are cooking, pour
oil into a heavy pan, heat, add
garlic, then add wine, cream,
pepper and basil. Stir and
reduce slightly.
When fillets are cooked, add to
mixture and leave for a minute
or two to allow some juices to
flavour the sauce.

SERVE

With sauteed potatoes and crisp
salad.

CHAR GRILLED KANGAROO FILLET WITH CRAB MEAT AND CHILLI SAUCE

4 fillets of kangaroo, about 200 gms each - 250 ml water -
2 tablespoons light soy sauce - 1 garlic clove, crushed -
1/2 cup of fresh crab meat - 1/2 cup sweet corn, drained -
2 small red chillies, chopped - 1 teaspoon cornflour mixed to a thin paste
with cold water

METHOD

Char grill fillets to desired state.
While fillets are cooking, pour
water and soy sauce into a heavy
pan, then add garlic, crab meat,
corn and chilli. Simmer gently.
Thicken with corn flour.
When fillets are cooked, place on
plate and cover with sauce.

SERVE

With Chinese egg noodles.

CHAR GRILLED KANGAROO FILLET WITH AVOCADO AND CALVADOS SAUCE

4 fillets of kangaroo, about 200 gms each - 30 ml Calvados -
250 ml fresh cream - 1 garlic clove, crushed - 1 large avocado, sliced -
1 tablespoon cashew nuts, crushed - 1 teaspoon fresh thyme -
black pepper to taste

METHOD

Char grill fillets to desired state.
While fillets are cooking, pour
cream into a heavy pan, then
add garlic, Calvados, cashew
nuts and pepper. Heat and
reduce slightly.
When fillets are cooked, add to
mixture, leave for a minute or
two to allow some juices to
flavour the sauce, then add
avocado.
Garnish with fresh thyme.

SERVE

With caraway noodles.

CHAR GRILLED KANGAROO FILLET WITH PIZZAIOLA SAUCE

4 fillets of kangaroo, about 200 gms each -
1 tablespoon extra virgin olive oil - 1 tablespoon Worcestershire sauce -
2 garlic cloves, crushed - 4 large ripe tomatoes, diced -
2 teaspoons fresh oregano - black pepper to taste

METHOD

Char grill fillets to desired state.
While fillets are cooking, pour
oil into a heavy pan, then add
garlic and heat gently while
stirring for 1 minute.
Add tomatoes, oregano and
black pepper, then simmer for
ten minutes. Mix in
Worcestershire sauce.
When fillets are cooked, add to
mixture, leave for a minute or
two to allow some juices to
flavour the sauce.

SERVE

With spaghetti.

CHAR GRILLED KANGAROO FILLET WITH BANANA AND WHITE RUM SAUCE

4 fillets of kangaroo, about 200 gms each - 1 tablespoon butter -
juice of 1 orange - 30 ml white rum - 1 banana, sliced thinly -
1 tablespoon brown sugar - 1/4 teaspoon ground cloves -
6 fresh mint leaves, sliced

METHOD

Char grill fillets to desired state.
While fillets are cooking, melt
butter in a heavy pan, then add
sugar and heat gently while
stirring. Add orange juice,
white rum, cloves and banana,
then mix and heat to reduce
slightly.
When fillets are cooked, serve
and cover with sauce.
Garnish with mint.

SERVE

With pilaf rice.

CHAR GRILLED KANGAROO FILLET WITH CRAB MEAT, CREAM AND SPRING ONION SAUCE

4 fillets of kangaroo, about 200 gms each - 250 ml fresh cream -
1 garlic clove, crushed - 1 / 2 cup fresh crab meat -
1 / 2 cup spring onions, sliced into rounds - 1 / 4 teaspoon saffron -
1 bunch fresh watercress

METHOD

Char grill fillets to desired state.
While fillets are cooking, heat
cream slightly in a heavy pan,
then add garlic, crab meat,
saffron and spring onions. Turn
heat up, and simmer gently to
reduce slightly.
When fillets are cooked, place
on plate and cover with sauce.
Garnish with watercress.

SERVE

With couscous.

CHAR GRILLED KANGAROO FILLET
WITH BAMBOO SHOOTS AND
SWEET AND SOUR SAUCE

4 fillets of kangaroo, about 200 gms each - 1 tablespoon peanut oil -
200 ml pineapple juice - 8 tablespoons tomato sauce -
2 dessertspoons light soy sauce - 1 garlic clove, crushed -
1 small onion, quartered - 1 small can bamboo shoots, drained -
1 teaspoon tamarind pulp - 2 pieces star anise

METHOD

Char grill fillets to desired state.
While fillets are cooking, heat
oil in a heavy pan, add onion,
garlic and star anise. Stir, then
mix in tomato sauce, tamarind
pulp, pineapple juice and soy
sauce.
Simmer for 5 minutes, stirring
frequently.
Add bamboo shoots and simmer
gently for a further 10 minutes.

SERVE

On bed of rice topped with
sauce as prepared.

CHAR GRILLED KANGAROO FILLET WITH YANDILLA MUSTARD SEED OIL MARINADE

4 fillets of kangaroo, about 200 gms each - 6 tablespoons Yandilla mustard seed oil (Another brand may be used if Yandilla is unavailable.) - 1 teaspoon cardamom seed, crushed - 1 teaspoon coriander seed, crushed - 1 teaspoon cummin seed, crushed - 1 teaspoon curry powder - lime pickle

METHOD

Cut a small hole in the centre of each fillet and fill with lime pickle.

Mix other ingredients and soak the kangaroo fillets in the marinade for at least four hours, turning to enable liquid to soak into the meat. Soaking overnight will ensure that full flavour is absorbed.

Char grill fillets to desired state.

SERVE

With saffron rice and fried onions.

CHAR GRILLED KANGAROO FILLET WITH PEANUT OIL AND SOY SAUCE MARINADE

4 fillets of kangaroo, about 200 gms each - 6 tablespoons peanut oil -
2 dessertspoons soy sauce - 4 teaspoons peanut butter

METHOD

Cut a small hole in the centre of each fillet and fill with peanut butter.

Mix other ingredients and soak the kangaroo fillets in the marinade for at least 4 hours, turning to enable liquid to soak into the meat. Soaking overnight will ensure full flavour is absorbed.

Char grill fillets to desired state.

SERVE

With rice or Chinese noodles and stir fry vegetables.

CHAR GRILLED KANGAROO FILLET WITH EXTRA VIRGIN OLIVE OIL MARINADE AND SUN-DRIED TOMATOES

4 fillets of kangaroo, about 200 gms each -
6 tablespoons extra virgin olive oil - 5 pieces of sun-dried tomatoes, chopped -
4 teaspoons pine nuts - 8 fresh basil leaves, chopped

METHOD

Cut small hole in the centre of each fillet and fill with chopped, sun-dried tomatoes, fresh basil and pine nuts.

Soak in olive oil for at least 4 hours, turning to enable liquid to soak into the meat. Soaking overnight will ensure full flavour is absorbed.

Char grill fillets to desired state.

SERVE

With rice or favourite pasta.

CHAR GRILLED KANGAROO FILLET WITH
LEMON JUICE, SAFFRON AND CHILLI

4 fillets of kangaroo, about 200 gms each -
6 tablespoons extra virgin olive oil - juice of 1 lemon -
1 garlic clove, crushed - 1 onion, finely diced - 1 capsicum, finely diced -
chilli, to taste - pinch of saffron - 2 teaspoons crushed, cummin seed

METHOD

Dice capsicum and onion, then
mix all ingredients except
fillets, olive oil and lemon juice.
Cut small hole in the centre of
each fillet and fill with some of
the mix.
Soak in the marinade, after
adding olive oil, for at least 4
hours, turning to enable liquid
to soak into the meat. Soaking
overnight will ensure full
flavour is absorbed.
Char grill fillets to desired state.

SERVE

With rice or cous cous.

CHAR GRILLED KANGAROO FILLET WITH BAY LEAF AND OLIVE OIL

4 fillets of kangaroo, about 200 gms each -
6 tablespoons extra virgin olive oil - 30 ml brandy -
1 garlic clove, crushed - 18 black olives, crushed - 10 capers, crushed -
4 bay leaves - 2 teaspoons fresh thyme

METHOD

Mix olive oil, brandy and bay leaves for marinade.
Mix other ingredients. Cut small hole in the centre of fillets and fill with crushed black olives, capers, thyme and garlic, then soak in the marinade for at least 4 hours, turning to enable liquid to soak into the meat. Soaking overnight will ensure full flavour is absorbed.
Char grill fillets to desired state.

SERVE

With rice or potatoes.

CHAR GRILLED KANGAROO FILLET WITH BLUE CHEESE AND PORT WINE MARINADE

*4 fillets of kangaroo, about 200 gms each - 6 tablespoons vegetable oil -
60 ml port wine - 4 teaspoons blue cheese - 4 prunes, chopped*

METHOD

Mix vegetable oil and port wine
for marinade.
Cut small hole in the centre of
each fillet and fill with blue
cheese and chopped prunes,
then soak in the marinade for at
least 4 hours, turning to enable
liquid to soak into the meat.
Soaking overnight will ensure
full flavour is absorbed.
Char grill fillets to desired state.

SERVE

With rice or potatoes.

CHAR GRILLED KANGAROO FILLET WITH AVOCADO, PRAWNS, FRESH LIME JUICE AND TEQUILA MARINADE

4 fillets of kangaroo, about 200 gms each - 6 tablespoons corn oil -
juice of 2 limes - 120 ml tequila - 1 / 2 avocado, chopped -
2 large cooked prawns, finely chopped

METHOD

Mix corn oil, lime juice and
tequila for marinade.
Soak meat in the marinade for
at least 4 hours, turning to
enable liquid to soak into the
meat. Soaking overnight will
ensure full flavour is absorbed.
Just before grilling, cut small
hole in the centre of each fillet
and fill with chopped prawns
and avocado.
Char grill fillets to desired state.

SERVE

With rice or fried potatoes.

CHAR GRILLED KANGAROO FILLET WITH FRESH PEACH AND SPARKLING WINE MARINADE

4 fillets of kangaroo, about 200 gms each - 6 tablespoons vegetable oil -
120 ml sparkling wine - 1 / 2 fresh peach, chopped -
4 teaspoons light mustard

METHOD

Mix vegetable oil and sparkling wine for marinade.
Cut small hole in the centre of each fillet and fill with peach and mustard, then soak in the marinade for at least 4 hours, turning to enable liquid to soak into the meat. Soaking overnight will ensure full flavour is absorbed.
Char grill fillets to desired state.

SERVE

With rice or potatoes.

ONE POT COOKING

Meat roasted on a bed of herbs and vegetables in a covered casserole is often referred to as a 'pot roast'. Indian curries are another well known form of single pot cooking. So is the humble 'Irish stew', at its best a creative mixture of meat and vegetables, flavoured by your choice of herbs and spices.

Single pot meals traditionally use cheap, 'braising' cuts, relying on the long, slow cooking process to tenderise the meats. Kangaroo rump and fillet, however, are cheap and all of our recipes use these prime cuts, minimising cooking time and producing a melt-in-the-mouth texture in the cooked meat.

If you decide to use gravy or braising cuts, cook the meal for at least twice as long and check that the meat is tender before serving.

Kangaroo proves its versatility in one pot cooking. We've adapted recipes from around the world. You'll think of more.

TAJINE OF KANGAROO WITH APRICOTS

*800 gms kangaroo rump or fillet, trimmed and diced -
6 tablespoons olive oil - 1 tablespoon butter - 1 tablespoon thick honey -
1 large onion, diced small - 10 dried apricots - 8 green olives, whole -
1 teaspoon saffron - 1 teaspoon ground cinnamon -
1 teaspoon ground cummin seed.*

METHOD

Heat olive oil and butter in heavy
pan, then add onion and saffron.
Fry until onion is transparent.
Add kangaroo meat, stir well and
cook for 1/2 to 3/4 of an hour
on medium heat, stirring often.
Add apricots, honey, olives,
cinnamon and cummin seed. Stir
well for 5 minutes until flavours
are combined.

SERVE

With couscous or rice.

KANGAROO CURRY WITH CINNAMON AND CLOVES

Note: This dish is best 1 to 2 days after cooking.

800 gms kangaroo rump or fillet, trimmed and diced - 6 tablespoons mustard seed oil (Yandilla is recommended) - 500 ml coconut milk, thin - 2 tablespoons tomato paste - 1 large onion, diced small - 6 fresh curry leaves (optional) - 3 teaspoons ground cloves - 4 cinnamon sticks - 2 teaspoons ground cardamom seeds - 2 teaspoons ground cummin seeds - 2 teaspoons ground coriander seeds - 2 teaspoons turmeric - 1 / 2 packet Kashmiri curry masala

METHOD

Heat mustard seed oil in heavy pan, then add onion and fry until transparent.

Add all herbs and spices, curry leaves and masala and fry for 2 to 3 minutes.

Add kangaroo meat, mix well and cook on medium heat, stirring often, for 5 minutes.

Add tomato paste, mix well, add coconut milk and stir together, then simmer for 1 hour.

SERVE

With Jasmine or Basmati rice and decorate with banana, yoghurt, lime pickle and pappadams.

CHILLI CON CARNE

500 gms kangaroo mince - 4 tablespoons olive or corn oil -
250 ml water - juice of 1 lime - 2 tablespoons tomato paste -
1 large onion, diced small - 1/2 capsicum, diced small -
1 can red kidney beans - fresh chilli to taste - 2 bay leaves -
2 dessertspoons finely chopped parsley - salt and pepper to taste

METHOD

Heat oil in heavy pan, then add onion, capsicum and bay leaves. Fry until onion is transparent. Add chilli and kangaroo and cook for 5 minutes on medium heat, stirring often. Add tomato paste and stir well. Add water and cook for 10 minutes, stirring often. Add kidney beans including liquid, stir and cook for a further 3 minutes or until beans are heated through. Add salt, pepper and chopped parsley.

SERVE

On bed of rice and sprinkle with lime juice.

BURGUNDY KANGAROO

800 gms kangaroo rump or fillet, trimmed and diced -
4 tablespoons olive oil - 300 ml burgundy - 2 garlic cloves, crushed -
1 large onion, diced small - 1 large carrot, sliced thickly -
2 rashers bacon, diced - 8 medium mushrooms, cut into quarters -
2 tablespoons flour - 2 bay leaves - 2 dessertspoons finely chopped, parsley

METHOD

Heat oil in heavy pan, then add onion, garlic, bacon, carrot and bay leaves. Cook for 4 minutes. Roll diced kangaroo pieces in flour and shake off excess. Place floured pieces in pan, stir, and add red wine and mushrooms. Cook on medium to low heat for 1/2 to 3/4 of an hour, stirring occasionally and adding more wine or water if mixture becomes dry.

Add parsley just before serving.

SERVE

With mashed or baked potato.

Note: This dish is best 1 to 2 days after cooking.

FRICASSEE OF KANGAROO

800 gms kangaroo rump or fillet, trimmed and diced -
2 tablespoons olive oil - 40 gms butter - 300 ml white wine -
200 ml water - 200 ml fresh cream - juice of 1 lemon -
2 garlic cloves, crushed - 1 small onion, diced small -
1 large carrot, sliced - 8 medium mushrooms, cut into quarters -
2 bay leaves - 2 dessertspoons finely chopped, tarragon -
1/4 teaspoon ground, black pepper - 1 heaped tablespoon of flour

METHOD

Heat oil in heavy pan, then add
onion, garlic, pepper, carrot and
bay leaves. Fry until onions are
transparent.
Add butter and meat, stir, then
mix in flour thoroughly. Slowly
add the water, lemon juice and
wine, stirring continually. Add
cream and mushrooms.
Simmer gently for 1 hour.
Just before serving, add
tarragon.

SERVE

With garlic buttered toast.

KANGAROO STEW

800 gms kangaroo rump or fillet, trimmed and diced -
2 tablespoons olive oil - 300 ml water - 2 tablespoons tomato paste -
2 garlic cloves, crushed - 1 large onion, quartered - 1 large carrot,
quartered and sliced - 1 stalk celery, sliced - 1 medium potato, diced small -
1 / 2 small leek, sliced - 2 tablespoons finely chopped, fresh parsley -
salt and pepper to taste

METHOD

Heat oil in heavy pan, then add onion and garlic. Fry until onions are transparent.

Add meat, stir and fry for 3 minutes. Add tomato paste and mix well, then add water. Stir thoroughly, add salt, pepper and vegetables.

Simmer gently for 45 minutes. Garnish with chopped parsley.

SERVE

With fried potatoes and cauliflower.

KANGAROO CALABRESE

800 gms kangaroo rump or fillet, trimmed and diced - 2 tablespoons olive oil -
150 ml water - 150 ml red wine - 2 tablespoons tomato paste -
2 garlic cloves, crushed - 1 large onion, quartered - 1 large tomato, diced -
8 whole black olives - 1 tablespoon chopped, fresh oregano - 1 tablespoon
finely chopped, fresh marjoram - 1 dessertspoon finely chopped, fresh basil -
1 / 2 teaspoon black pepper, ground

METHOD

Heat oil in heavy pan, then add
onion and garlic. Fry until onions
are transparent.
Add meat, stir and fry for 2 to
3 minutes, then add tomato
paste, mix well, and add wine
and water. Stir thoroughly, add
pepper, oregano, marjoram,
tomato and olives.
Simmer gently for 45 minutes.
Garnish with chopped basil.

SERVE

With crusty Italian bread.

GREEN KANGAROO CURRY

800 gms kangaroo rump or fillet, trimmed and diced -
2 tablespoons mustard seed oil (Yandilla brand is recommended) -
300 ml thin coconut milk - 2 tablespoons light soy sauce -
2 garlic cloves, crushed - 8 snow peas - 1 / 2 cup creamed coconut, grated -
2 dessertspoons toasted, threaded coconut - 1 spring onion, chopped -
1 small green chilli, chopped - 1 / 2 teaspoon cardamom seed, ground -
1 / 2 teaspoon cummin seed, ground - 1 / 2 teaspoon coriander seed, ground -
lots fresh coriander, chopped - lots fresh sweet basil, chopped -
2 tablespoons chopped, fresh mint - 1 stalk lemon grass, finely sliced

METHOD

Heat oil in heavy pan, then add garlic, coriander seed, cummin seed, cardamom seed and lemon grass. Stir over low heat for about 1 minute, then add roo meat. Fry on medium heat for 3 minutes while stirring.
Add coconut milk and soy sauce, mix well then add fresh herbs and chilli.
Simmer gently for 45 minutes.

Just before serving thicken with grated coconut.
Garnish with snow peas, spring onion and toasted coconut.

SERVE

With Jasmine rice.

KANGAROO GOULASH

800 gms kangaroo rump or fillet, trimmed and diced -
1 tablespoon lard (2 tablespoons of olive oil can be used instead) -
100 ml water - 100 ml dry white wine - 100 ml sour cream -
2 garlic cloves, crushed - 1 large onion, quartered - 1 large tomato, diced -
2 tablespoons paprika - 1 tablespoon plain flour -
1 tablespoon finely chopped, fresh parsley - salt to taste

METHOD

Heat oil in heavy pan, then add
onion and garlic. Fry until onions
are transparent.
Add meat, stir, and fry for 3
minutes, then add paprika, flour
and tomato. Mix well, then add
wine and water.
Stir thoroughly, add sour cream
and salt, stir and simmer gently
for 45 minutes.
Garnish with fresh parsley.

SERVE

With dumplings or spaezli.

KANGAROO WITH PERNOD
AND FRESH FENNEL

800 gms kangaroo rump or fillet, trimmed and diced -
2 tablespoons extra virgin olive oil - 200 ml water - 150 ml Pernod -
2 tablespoons fresh cream - 2 garlic cloves, crushed -
1 small bulb fresh fennel, quartered

METHOD

Marinate kangaroo meat in
Pernod for a minimum of two
hours, overnight is best.
Heat oil in heavy pan, then add
garlic and meat. Stir and cook
for 3 minutes.
Add cream and water, mix
well, then add fennel.
Simmer gently for 45 minutes.

SERVE

With broccoli and fresh tomato
and onion salad.

PIES AND PASTRIES

There's nothing so Australian as a pie.

Pies are easily prepared at home and make a filling and nutritious meal. There are many variations on the theme of the standard Aussie beef pie, and kangaroo is often the perfect meat to use.

Here we provide recipes based on the traditional British steak-and-kidney and cottage pies, and show how kangaroo can lift the flavour of a Greek spinach-and-fetta-cheese pastry. Chinese spring rolls, Indian samosas and North African boureks can all be made successfully with roo meat. Your imagination is the limit.

Pies and pastries can be eaten immediately or stored in the refrigerator or freezer until hunger strikes or the kids start grumbling.

Try some of these recipes, then create your own pies and pastries, using what you've learned about how roo tastes with different vegetables, herbs and spices.

KANGAROO COTTAGE PIE

500 gms kangaroo mince - 2 tablespoons lard or oil -
1 tablespoon Worcestershire sauce - 300 ml water or 1 / 2 and 1 / 2 stout
and water mix - 8 teaspoons butter - 2 tablespoons tomato paste -
1 onion, finely diced - 2 rashers bacon, finely diced - 3 medium potatoes -
1 large carrot, grated - 2 tablespoons finely chopped, parsley

METHOD

Heat oven to 180 degrees.
Boil and mash the potatoes.
Heat lard or oil in heavy pan,
then add onion and bacon. Fry
until onion is transparent.
Add mince and carrot and cook
for 4 minutes, stirring well.
Mix in tomato paste, add water,
Worcestershire sauce and
parsley. Cook for 4 minutes,
stirring all the time.
Transfer mixture to casserole
dish, top with mashed potato,
and dot surface with butter.
Cook in oven, at 180 degrees,
for 20 minutes, or until potato
is crisp and brown on the
surface.

SERVE

With peas and stir-fried cabbage
with caraway seeds.

KANGAROO AND KIDNEY PIE

500 gms kangaroo rump or fillet, diced - 4 lambs' kidneys, diced -
2 tablespoons vegetable oil - 150 ml water - 150 ml bitter beer -
2 garlic cloves, crushed - 1 onion, finely diced -
1 medium carrot, cut into rounds - 1 small tomato, thinly sliced -
2 tablespoons finely chopped, parsley - 2 bay leaves -
salt and pepper to taste - 1 packet puff pastry - 1/2 cup wholemeal flour

METHOD

Heat oven to 175 degrees.
Roll kangaroo pieces in a little wholemeal flour.
Heat oil in heavy pan, add onion, garlic and carrot, and fry until onions are transparent.
Add roo and kidneys, and cook for 4 minutes, stirring well.
Add water and beer, stir, then add bay leaves, salt, pepper and parsley. Simmer gently for 30 minutes, stirring occasionally.

Transfer mixture to casserole dish and top with sliced tomato.
Cover with pastry, prepared as per directions on packet.
Cook in oven at 175 degrees for 15 minutes.

SERVE

With peas and mashed potatoes.

KANGAROO, VEGETABLE AND WALNUT PIE

500 gms kangaroo rump or fillet, diced - 2 tablespoons vegetable oil -
300 ml water - 1 dessertspoon tomato paste - 2 garlic cloves, crushed -
1 onion, quartered - 1 small carrot, diced - 1/2 large potato, diced small -
1/2 stick celery, sliced - 1/4 cup walnut pieces - 1/4 cup diced turnip -
2 prunes, sliced - 1 tablespoon fresh, finely chopped thyme -
2 bay leaves - salt and pepper to taste
Pastry 250 gms plain flour - 200 gms butter - 60 ml cold water

METHOD

Heat oven to 175 degrees.

Heat oil in heavy pan, add onion, garlic and all vegetables then fry for 3 minutes while stirring. Add meat and cook for 4 minutes, stirring well.

Add tomato paste, stir, and add water, mixing well. Add bay leaves, salt, pepper and thyme, then simmer gently for 30 minutes, stirring occasionally.

Stir in prunes and walnuts, and let mixture cool while preparing pastry.

PASTRY

Rub butter through flour with fingers until it resembles bread crumbs (not too fine), add water and carefully combine ingredients until a dough is formed.

Roll out until desired thickness and size is obtained.

Lay the dough in a pie dish. Spoon in cooled filling and cover with rolled pastry top.

Cook in oven at 175 degrees for 15 minutes, or until pastry is browned.

SERVE With broccoli and green beans.

KANGAROO, GOAT'S CHEESE, ROAST CAPSICUM AND SHERRY PIE

500 gms kangaroo rump or fillet, diced - 2 tablespoons olive oil -
150 ml water - 150 ml dry sherry - 1 dessertspoon tomato paste -
2 garlic cloves, crushed - 1 onion, finely chopped - 1 medium capsicum -
2 dessertspoons goats' cheese, crumbled - 1 dessertspoon fresh, finely
chopped, thyme - 2 bay leaves - salt and pepper to taste
Pastry *250 gms plain flour - 200 gms butter - 60 ml cold water*

METHOD

Heat oven to 200 degrees. Place capsicum on lightly-oiled tray, and bake until skin is blackened. Remove from oven, peel skin from flesh while still warm, then dice. Heat oil in heavy pan, add onion and garlic. Fry for 3 minutes while stirring. Add meat and cook for 3 minutes, stirring well. Add tomato paste, stir, then mix in water and sherry. Add bay leaves, salt and pepper, diced capsicum and thyme. Simmer gently for 30 minutes, stirring occasionally.

Fold goats' cheese into mixture, then allow to cool while preparing pastry.

PASTRY

Rub butter through flour with fingers until it resembles bread crumbs (not too fine), add water, and carefully combine ingredients until a dough is formed. Roll out until desired thickness and size is obtained. Lay in a pie dish, and spoon in cooled filling. Cover with rolled pastry top. Cook in oven at 175 degrees for 15 minutes, or until pastry is browned.

SERVE With crisp green salad dressed with olive oil and balsamic vinegar.

KANGAROO WELLINGTON

500 gms kangaroo rump or fillet - 2 tablespoons olive oil -
1 garlic clove, crushed - 1 onion, finely diced -
4 small mushrooms, very finely chopped -
1 small tomato, very finely diced - 1 / 2 cup fresh watercress -
1 packet puff pastry - 1 egg

METHOD

Heat oven to 200 degrees.
Heat oil in heavy pan, add roo
meat and sear all over. Remove
from pan, and allow to cool.
Mash onion, garlic, mushrooms
and tomato.
Prepare puff pastry as per
directions on packet, roll into flat
sheet and spread centre of sheet
with mashed mushroom mixture.
Lay meat on top of mixture and
join pastry around meat.

Turn over onto lightly oiled
baking tray so that pastry join is
on underside.
Beat egg in a bowl, then brush
pastry with beaten egg and cook
in pre-heated oven for 20
minutes, or until pastry is golden
brown. Garnish with watercress.

SERVE

With boiled potatoes and string
beans.

SPICED KANGAROO SAMOSA

300 gms kangaroo mince -
1 tablespoon mustard seed oil (Yandilla brand is recommended) -
1 tablespoon tomato paste - 1 garlic clove, crushed -
1 / 2 onion, finely diced - 1 / 2 cup fresh peas -
1 / 4 teaspoon cummin seed, ground - 1 / 4 teaspoon cardamom seed, ground -
1 / 4 teaspoon coriander seed, ground - 1 / 2 teaspoon curry powder -
1 tablespoon fresh, finely chopped, coriander - 1 packet puff pastry - 1 egg

METHOD

Heat oven to 200 degrees. Heat oil in heavy pan, then add cummin, cardamom, coriander seed and curry powder. Fry gently for 1 minute while stirring, then add onions, garlic, peas and meat. Stir, add tomato paste, stir again, and fry gently for 4 minutes. Remove from heat, add fresh coriander, and allow to cool. Prepare puff pastry as per directions on packet, roll into flat sheet, and cut into 15 cm diameter rounds.

Spoon filling onto rounds, brush edges of pastry with a little cold water, then fold two opposite edges to centre, pinching lengthways to join. Repeat for each samosa.

Beat egg in a bowl, then brush pastry with beaten egg, and cook in preheated oven until pastry is golden brown.

SERVE

With crisp lettuce and chutney.

KANGAROO, SPINACH, FETTA CHEESE AND BLACK OLIVE STRUDEL

300 gms kangaroo mince - 1 dessertspoon olive oil - 2 tablespoons butter -
1 teaspoon ouzo - 1 tablespoon tomato paste - 1 garlic clove, crushed -
1/2 onion, finely diced - 4 small, fresh spinach leaves, finely chopped -
2 tablespoons fetta cheese, crumbled - 1/4 cup black olives, pitted and diced -
1 teaspoon oregano - ground black pepper to taste - 1 packet Filo pastry

METHOD

Heat oven to 200 degrees.

Heat oil in heavy pan, add onions, garlic and meat, stir, and fry for 3 minutes. Stir in tomato paste. Add ouzo, spinach, olives, pepper and oregano, stir, and fry for another 4 minutes.

Remove from heat, add fetta cheese and cool.

Melt butter in separate pan.

Prepare eight sheets of Filo pastry as per directions on packet, brushing alternate sheets with melted butter, then spoon filling along centre of pastry, leaving space to fold at either end. Turn ends inward, brush exposed surfaces with melted butter and shape into a roll.

Turn over onto lightly oiled baking tray so that pastry join is on underside, brush top with melted butter, and bake in preheated oven for 30 minutes, or until crisp.

SERVE

With Greek salad.

KANGAROO BOUREKS

300 gms kangaroo mince - 1 dessertspoon olive oil - 2 tablespoons butter -
juice of 1 fresh lime - 2 garlic cloves, crushed -
2 dessertspoons almond paste - 1 teaspoon finely chopped, fresh mint -
2 teaspoons finely chopped, fresh coriander -
1/4 teaspoon ground black pepper - 1 packet Filo pastry

METHOD

Heat oven to 200 degrees.
Heat oil in heavy pan, add garlic and meat, stir, and fry for 5 minutes. Turn heat down, add almond paste and mix well. Add pepper, coriander, mint and lime juice, and stir until combined. Melt butter in separate pan. Prepare 8 sheets of Filo pastry as per directions on packet, brushing alternate sheets with melted butter. Cut into approximately 12 cm diameter rounds to make one bourek per person.

Place wrapped boureks on lightly-oiled baking tray so that pastry joins are on the underside, brush tops with melted butter, and bake in preheated oven until crisp.

SERVE

With slices of orange sprinkled with cinnamon and sugar.

Boureks served in this manner make a perfect entree.

KANGAROO SPRING ROLLS

200 gms kangaroo rump or fillet, sliced into very thin strips -
1 dessertspoon light soy sauce - 1 garlic clove, crushed -
1/2 cup cooked rice - 1 medium carrot, grated -
1/2 stick celery, shredded - 1/2 cup chopped, bean sprouts - 2 teaspoons
finely chopped, fresh coriander - 2 teaspoons crushed, pickled pink ginger -
1 packet spring roll wrappers - 500 gms Frymaster or similar cooking oil

METHOD

Heat oil in deep fryer or heavy
pan until it bubbles when a
piece of chopped bean sprout is
dropped into it.
While oil is heating, combine all
ingredients in a bowl.
Spoon mixture onto individual
spring roll wrappers, and fold as
per directions on packet.
Deep fry in hot oil until
cooked.

SERVE

With favourite dipping sauce
and pickled cucumbers.

FIERY KANGAROO AND PRAWN ROLLS

200 gms kangaroo mince - 4 large cooked prawns, sliced into thin rounds -
1 dessertspoon light soy sauce - 1 garlic clove, crushed - 1/2 cup, fine,
cooked egg noddles - 1 cup fresh, thinly sliced, cabbage - 3 fresh small red
chillies, finely chopped - 2 teaspoons fresh, finely chopped, Vietnamese mint -
2 teaspoons fresh, finely chopped, sweet basil - 1 packet Spring Roll wrappers -
500 gms Frymaster or similar cooking oil

METHOD

Heat oil in deep fryer or heavy
pan until it bubbles when a
piece of egg noodle is dropped
into it.
Mix all ingredients except oil
and spring roll wrappers.
Spoon mixture onto individual
spring roll wrappers, and fold as
per directions on packet.
Deep fry in hot oil for 3
minutes, or until cooked.

SERVE

With cucumber, garlic and
yoghurt dip and prawn crackers.

CHILDREN'S MEALS

Cooking for children is a never-ending battle to provide nourishment and flavour with inexpensive ingredients and never enough time.

Roo is a versatile and tasty alternative to other meat and is far less expensive than any of its competitors. It is high in nutrition, very low in fat, and adds flavour to innumerable dishes.

Here are recipes that offer your children new tastes in familiar guises and old favourites they will love. Best of all, most take less than an hour to prepare. They will provide food for four hungry children and, if the children are young or have small appetites, will include leftovers for school lunchboxes or snacks.

TROPICAL ROO BURGER

500 gms kangaroo mince - 1 tablespoon vegetable oil -
1/2 cup fresh bread crumbs - 1 egg - 1/2 small banana, mashed -
6 crushed macadamia nuts - 2 dessertspoons chopped, fresh mint -
pinch of salt and pepper

METHOD

Mix all ingredients together in a bowl and shape into flat, round patties. If mixture does not hold together, more breadcrumbs may be added.

Heat oil in a heavy pan, and pan fry to taste, turning often to ensure even cooking. The burgers are cooked when outside is browned and they have minimal resistance when pressed with spatula.

SERVE

Between crusty bread rolls with pineapple, coconut, avocado, tomato and/or lettuce as desired.

Note: For adults 30 mls of dark rum can be added to mixture and the burgers served with cold rum drinks.

KANGAROO TACOS

500 gms kangaroo mince - 2 tablespoons corn oil - 250 ml water -
2 dessertspoons tomato paste - 1/2 onion, diced small -
1/2 capsicum, diced small - 6 mint leaves, finely chopped -
salt and pepper to taste - 4 large taco shells -
shredded lettuce - grated cheese

METHOD

Heat oil in heavy saucepan or frying pan, then add onion and capsicum. Fry until onion is transparent.

Add mince, then mix well while cooking for 4 minutes.

Add tomato paste, mix well then add water. Stir in and cook for about 10 minutes or until the mixture is thick. Stir in mint leaves, salt and pepper.

Heat taco shells as per instructions on packet. Place shredded lettuce inside, spoon in meat mix and top with grated cheese.

SERVE

With three bean mix or red kidney beans.

KANGAROO KEBABS

*300 gms kangaroo fillet, cut into cubes - 1 onion, quartered - 1 capsicum,
cut to same size pieces as onion - 1 banana, thickly sliced -
2 rashers of bacon, cut into squares - 4 bamboo skewers*

METHOD

Thread ingredients onto
skewers. Grill, barbecue or fry
in a heavy pan, with a little oil,
for about 8 minutes. Turn often
to ensure even cooking.

SERVE

On a bed of rice and top with
sauce of your choice.

MEATBALLS IN TOMATO SAUCE

500 gms kangaroo mince - 2 tablespoons olive oil - 500 ml water -
8 tablespoons tomato paste - 1 garlic clove, crushed -
1/2 onion, finely chopped - 1/2 cup bread crumbs - 1 egg -
1 dessertspoon finely chopped, fresh oregano or marjoram leaves -
8 fresh basil leaves, finely chopped - salt and pepper to taste

METHOD

Mix kangaroo mince, onion, garlic, basil, breadcrumbs and egg thoroughly in a bowl, then shape mixture into balls.

Heat olive oil in heavy pan, then add onion. Fry until transparent, then add garlic and oregano or marjoram.

Add tomato paste and mix well. Add water and stir into mixture. Cook slowly for about 2 hours, adding more water if required.

Add meatballs and cook for another 1/2 an hour.

Add salt and pepper.

SERVE

With favourite pasta.

KANGAROO MINCE ON TOAST

500 gms kangaroo mince - 2 tablespoons vegetable oil -
1 tablespoon tomato paste - 1 / 2 cup of water - 1 / 2 onion, finely chopped -
1 carrot, thinly sliced - 1 small potato, diced small - 1 / 2 cup of fresh
peas (frozen can be used) - 1 tablespoon chopped parsley

METHOD

Heat oil in heavy pan. Add
onions, carrot and potato, and
fry for 4 minutes
Add kangaroo mince, stir until
mince is cooked through. Add
tomato paste and mix well.
Add water, peas and parsley,
stir and cook on a medium heat
for about 5 minutes, or until
mixture is thick.

SERVE

On buttered toast.

KANGAROO BURGERS

500 gms kangaroo mince - 1 tablespoon vegetable oil -
1/2 onion, finely chopped - 1/2 cup breadcrumbs - 1 egg -
1 tablespoon chopped parsley - salt and pepper to taste

METHOD

Mix all ingredients together and
shape into desired size burgers.
7 cms in diameter and 3 cms
thick is a good guide.
Heat oil in a heavy pan and fry,
turning often to ensure even
cooking.
The burgers are cooked when
outside is browned and they
have minimal resistance when
pressed with spatula.

SERVE

With mashed or fried potatoes
or in bread rolls.

KANGAROO BOLOGNESE

500 gms kangaroo mince - 2 tablespoons olive oil -
2 dessertspoons tomato paste - 250 ml water - 1/2 onion, finely chopped -
1 rasher bacon, finely diced - 2 dessertspoons, finely chopped parsley -
salt and pepper to taste

METHOD

Heat oil in heavy pan, then add
onion and bacon. Fry until
onion is transparent.
Add kangaroo mince and cook
for 5 minutes.
Add tomato paste, mix well,
then mix in water.
Cook for about 10 minutes, or
until mixture is thick.
Add parsley, salt and pepper.

SERVE

With favourite pasta.

KANGAROO SCHNITZEL

4 pieces thin kangaroo fillet - 1 tablespoon vegetable oil -
1 cup breadcrumbs - 1/2 cup flour - 1/2 cup milk

METHOD

Coat meat in flour. Dip in milk,
then coat with breadcrumbs.
Fry in pan with vegetable oil
until golden brown.

SERVE

With fried or mashed potatoes
and sauce of your choice.

KANGAROO SUMMER SALAD

300 gms kangaroo fillet cooked to desired state -
rare to medium is best - 10 mixed lettuce leaves, shredded -
2 Lebanese cucumbers, quartered lengthways -
small tin pineapple pieces, drained - small tin bamboo shoots, drained -
1 large carrot cut into thin strips - large handful bean sprouts -
2 dessertspoons sesame seeds, toasted

METHOD

Slice cooked kangaroo fillets
thinly.
Mix all other ingredients, except
sesame seeds, in a large bowl.
Decorate with sliced kangaroo
and sprinkle with sesame seeds.

SERVE

With salad dressing.

CREATIVE KANGAROO SANDWICHES AND ROLLS

Thinly sliced, cooked and cooled kangaroo fillets -
peanut butter and lettuce - red currant jelly and cucumber -
avocado and cream cheese - garlic butter, tomato and chopped, fresh basil -
riccotta cheese and alfalfa sprouts - vegemite and carrots -
small packet of potato or corn chips - cold, sliced potato, tomato pickle
and chopped, fresh parsley - beetroot, onion and chopped mint -
thinly sliced apple and mayonnaise

SERVE

In your favourite bread or rolls.

Note: All fillings can be mixed
and matched as you desire.

GLOSSARY

BOUREK	North African pastry parcel
CALVADOS	French apple brandy
HARIRA	Thick, North African lentil soup
PILAF RICE	Rice, slow cooked in a covered pot
SPAEZLI	Tiny, pan-fried dumplings
SAMOSA	Indian pastry parcel

AVAILABLE IN MOST SPECIALTY FOOD STORES

COUSCOUS	Fine grained semolina
COS LETTUCE	Long leaved lettuce of Mediterranean origin
NATIVE PEPPER LEAF	Leaf of Australian pepper tree
ROSELLA FLOWERS	Flower from the native Australian Rosella plant
YANDILLA MUSTARD SEED OIL	Cold pressed, cholesterol-free oil made in Australia

AVAILABLE IN MOST ITALIAN FOOD STORES

PANCETTA	Italian-style salted pork
PECORINO CHEESE	Italian hard cheese

AVAILABLE IN MOST ASIAN FOOD STORES

CANDLENUTS Asian nut, similar to a macadamia nut in shape, size and texture

CURRY LEAVES The leaf of the curry bush

LAKSA MINT Peppery-tasting Asian herb

PAPPADAMS Traditional Indian lentil wafer

STAR ANISE Asian spice

VIETNAMESE MINT Asian herb

TYPES OF PASTA USED

FETTUCINI Thin strips of wheat and egg pasta

FUSILLI Spiral shaped wheat and egg pasta

PENNE Short, tubular wheat and egg pasta

PASTINI Tiny, granular wheat and egg pasta

TAGLIATELLE As fettucini, but slightly larger

VERMICELLI Fine strands of wheat and egg pasta

INDEX

CHAR GRILLED KANGAROO

INDEX

CHILDREN'S MEALS

ONE POT COOKING

INDEX

PASTA DISHES

PIES AND PASTRIES

INDEX

INDEX